ENERGY
**Now and in
the Future**

Water Power

Neil Morris

A⁺
Smart Apple Media

Smart Apple Media
P.O. Box 3263
Mankato, MN 56002

Printed in the United States

Library of Congress Cataloging-in-Publication Data

Morris, Neil, 1946-
  Water power / by Neil Morris.
      p. cm. -- (Energy now and in the future)
  Includes index.
  Summary: "Discusses ways we can get power from water by damming rivers
or harnessing tides and ocean waves, and how water power may be used in the
future"--Provided by publisher.
  ISBN 978-1-59920-343-0 (hbk.)
  1. Water-power--Juvenile literature. I. Title.
  TC146.M67 2009
  333.91'4--dc22
                                                                    2008038729

Designed by Helen James
Edited by Mary-Jane Wilkins
Artwork by Guy Callaby
Picture research by Su Alexander

Photograph acknowledgements
Page 9 Rick Doyle/Corbis; 11 Hubert Stadler/Corbis; 12 Bettmann/Corbis;
13 Colin Garratt: Milepost 92 1/2/Corbis; 15 Lester Lefkowitz/Corbis; 17 Gilles
Sabrie/Corbis; 18 epa/Corbis; 19 Richard Cummins/Corbis; 21 Adam Hart-Davis/
Science Photo Library; 24 Yann Arthus-Bertrand/Corbis; 27 NASA/Corbis;
28 James Leynse/Corbis; 32 Ocean Power Technologies, Inc; 33 Earth-Vision.Biz/
Wave Dragon; 39 NELHA; 40 NASA/Corbis; 42 Hiroshi Hiquchi/Photolibrary;
43 AFP/Getty Images
Front cover James Davis/Eye Ubiquitous/Corbis

9 8 7 6 5 4 3 2 1

Contents

Power from a Vital Resource

Water is a vitally important resource to all of us on Earth. The planet's oceans and seas cover more than two-thirds of its surface. All living things need to drink water to live, and water is also a valuable source of renewable energy. We can use it to provide the power to work machines and to light and heat our homes, offices, and factories.

An Endless Sequence

The world's water moves around the planet in a never-ending sequence called the hydrological, or water, cycle. About 97 percent of Earth's water is in the oceans. The rest is in lakes and rivers, or locked as ice in polar ice caps and glaciers.

As the Sun heats the oceans, water evaporates, changes into a gas called water vapor, and rises into the atmosphere. As it rises, the vapor cools and condenses, forming tiny droplets of water that join together to make clouds. Eventually, the water falls back to Earth as precipitation—rain, snow, or some other form of moisture—and most of it lands back in the oceans. Some water lands on the ground and is taken up by plants. The rest forms streams and rivers that carry the water back to the oceans. When that water evaporates, the water cycle starts over again.

The Power of Movement

Water creates power when it flows from one place to another. Rivers create power naturally, as they flow toward the sea. The water flows from higher to lower ground, usually from hills or mountains down to sea level.

The 3,900 mile (6,300 km) long Chang Jiang River begins in the snow-covered mountains of western China. Its source is a glacier more than 3 miles (5,000 m) above sea level. This means the river moves downhill at an

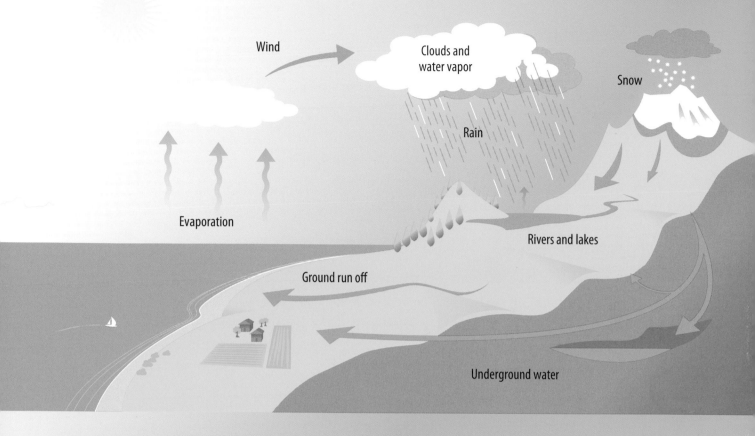

Wind

Clouds and
water vapor

Snow

Rain

Evaporation

Rivers and lakes

Ground run off

Underground water

average rate of 31 inches per 0.6 miles (80 cm per km). Hydroelectric dams have been built and are planned on the Chang Jiang (see page 18). By comparison, the Thames River in England drops 600 feet (183 m) over its 221 mile (356 km) course from the Cotswold Hills to the sea. This is an average rate of 21 inches (53 cm) per 0.6 miles (1 km).

The water cycle is a never-ending process. It is driven by energy from the Sun, which heats water and air, creating clouds and wind.

What Is Renewable Energy?

The water cycle ensures that Earth's water resources are constantly recycled. This makes water a renewable resource, because it can be used again and again and is not in danger of running out. There is a lot of discussion about the importance of renewable energy sources in the media today. These sources of energy are crucial because they are always there and using them does not create waste gases that pollute the atmosphere. Biomass, geothermal, solar, and wind power are the other renewable forms of energy. Fossil fuels (coal, oil, and natural gas) and nuclear power (which uses uranium) are nonrenewable.

The Force of the Tides

Water in the world's oceans also moves naturally. There are several forces at work. The first is the gravitational pull of the moon, which creates the rise and fall in the oceans' water level that we call tides. The pull on Earth is strongest on the side nearest the moon and weakest on the side farthest from it. This stretches the oceans so they bulge up in a high tide on both sides of Earth. Water is always moving between high and low tide. This movement can create electricity (see page 22).

Swirling Ocean Currents

The world's winds can disturb ocean waters at the surface and to a depth of about 328 feet (100 m). This creates currents that may flow for thousands of miles or kilometers. Wind-driven currents move in giant circles, called gyres. At greater depths, currents are caused by differences in water temperature and salinity (saltiness). Cold water from the poles sinks toward the seabed and moves toward the equator, where it warms up and rises again. This pattern is called thermohaline circulation.

Moving Water in Waves

We are all familiar with the movement of waves at the seashore. Waves are caused by wind blowing across the surface of the ocean. It looks as though the water moves across the surface of the ocean,

Measuring Water Flow

The water in rivers moves at different rates. Scientists measure the volume of water that flows past a particular point in a certain amount of time. This is called discharge. It is measured in cusecs (cubic feet per second) or cumecs (cubic meters per second). This measurement varies depending on rainfall and other conditions. It also varies between rivers.

River	Discharge	
Amazon	6,355,800 cusecs	(180,000 cumecs)
Chang Jiang	769,758 cusecs	(21,800 cumecs)
Rhine	77,682 cusecs	(2,200 cumecs)
Thames	2,013 cusecs	(57 cumecs)

Where Did Water First Come From?

Earth formed about 4,600 million years ago from a collection of debris spinning around a new star, the Sun. The planet began as a red-hot, semimolten ball. As Earth cooled, its surface was covered with volcanoes, which spewed out molten rock, dust, and gases. These included steam formed by the chemicals combining beneath Earth's surface. The steam condensed into water droplets in Earth's atmosphere of gases, falling back to the surface. Over millions of years, the water collected into huge pools that eventually became one large ocean. The water in the ocean began to evaporate, starting the water cycle.

but the water in waves actually stays in approximately the same place, moving around in circles. Ocean waves move in the same way as a rope when you whip it up and down. A wave moves along the rope, but the rope itself does not move forward. When an ocean wave nears land, it starts to drag on the bottom. Waves become closer together and taller, then the water moves forward as the wave breaks.

Surfers understand the surging movement of waves and their tremendous power.

From Waterwheels to Locomotives

Water was probably first used to produce mechanical power about 2,500 years ago, in the ancient Egyptian city of Alexandria. Around that time, scientists and inventors found that they could use waterwheels to drive mills.

The mills ground grain into flour. In later centuries, waterwheels drove bellows, mechanical hammers, and looms for making textiles. Along with windmills, waterwheels were the main suppliers of power until the steam engine was developed in the eighteenth century.

Water Power in Ancient Times

The earliest written reference to a water mill was around 85 B.C. The mill was mentioned by an ancient Greek poet, who celebrated the fact that young women would no longer have to grind corn by hand. According to the ancient Greek geographer Strabo, the Anatolian King Mithradates VI was using some form of water machine just 20 years later. Around 25 B.C., the Roman engineer Vitruvius wrote a handbook for architects. He described an undershot waterwheel, which was turned by water flowing along a chute at the base of the waterwheel.

Harnessing the Power of Water

The ancient Romans were experts at diverting water through aqueducts. During the fourth century A.D., they diverted water from a river near Arles in Roman Gallia (present-day southern France) so that it poured downhill and drove eight pairs of water mills.

Turning the Wheel

The earliest water mills had a vertical shaft that drove millstones. These were followed by mills with a horizontal shaft, driven by a wheel in an upright position. In overshot mills, the water flowed along a channel and poured over the top of the wheel into scoops or buckets. The force of the falling water turned the wheel. Undershot mills were not efficient as the water pushed the wheel from below.

This old waterwheel is still doing its work at a German mill.

The mills produced 4.4 tons (4 t) of flour a day, which was enough to feed the local town of 12,500 people.

Many hundreds of years later, in 1769, the British manufacturer Richard Arkwright (1732–92) invented a spinning machine that made cotton thread for the textile industry. He opened a cotton mill by a channel of water flowing from the Derwent River, and all the machines—called water frames—were driven by a waterwheel.

Why Not Use Waterwheels Today?

We could use waterwheels for milling and other purposes, but they are less efficient and powerful than other sources of energy. James Watt (1736–1819) built the first steam-powered flour mill in 1780. During the twentieth century, steam was replaced by electricity. Today, flour is generally milled between electrically powered steel rollers rather than stones. Manufacturers find electricity a more reliable, constant source of energy. Mills can be located anywhere, not necessarily near running water. However, some nineteenth-century mills have been renovated and still successfully produce stone-ground flour.

Watt's Engine

A steam engine works by turning liquid water into gaseous steam and then turning it back into water again. A fire in a boiler, which usually burns coal, boils water. The resulting steam enters a cylinder and quickly cools and condenses. This leaves a vacuum into which a piston inside the cylinder moves. The moving piston is connected to a beam that also moves up and down and uses a cogwheel to connect with a large wheel and turn it. The wheel can then be connected by cogs and gears to other equipment.

An original Watt steam engine

Steam Takes Over

In the same year that Arkwright invented his water frame, 1769, Scottish engineer James Watt produced an improved version of a machine that was becoming increasingly popular—the steam engine. This type of engine had first been developed in 1712 by Thomas Newcomen, but Watt's version used less coal and produced more power. It did this by using a condenser to change steam back into water by cooling it. In 1782, Watt developed a double-action machine that used steam to push a piston in opposite directions.

The Coming of Railroads

Steam power created the age of railroads, which started in the early nineteenth century in Britain. In 1830, a steam locomotive called *Rocket* pulled a train to mark the opening of the Liverpool and

Heroic Beginnings

Hero was a Greek scientist and inventor who lived in the Roman-controlled Egyptian city of Alexandria around A.D. 10–70. He invented a steam engine, called an *aeolipile*, that consisted of a hollow globe attached by pipes to a steam kettle. Two open pipes were attached to the globe, and when steam rushed out of these, the globe turned. Hero used his invention as a scientific demonstration toy and as a device to open temple doors.

A steam locomotive fills its tender with water at a stop in Spain.

Manchester Railway. *Rocket* had a top speed of 29 miles (47 km) per hour, but faster engines were soon introduced. The locomotives had tenders behind the steam engine that carried supplies of coal and water. Railroad stations had large tanks of water, so that the tenders and boilers could be regularly refilled.

Today's Steam Engines

Modern versions of Watt's engine use high-pressure and superheated steam to make them more powerful. Some still operate, including steam locomotives in China and India. More importantly, today we use a different type of steam engine to make electricity. This is the steam turbine, which produces a rotary motion when steam spins bladed wheels. In modern power stations, the water is boiled by burning coal, gas, or oil, or by nuclear fission (in nuclear reactors) or by using biomass, geothermal, or solar power.

Damming Rivers

Hydroelectricity, or hydropower, is electricity generated by the power of moving water. The terms usually describe a power-generating system based on a dam built across a river. Such power plants have been built since the end of the nineteenth century.

The first was built in 1882 on the Fox River in Wisconsin. The electricity powered trams in a nearby town. Other systems were used for electric lighting. By 1895, the powerful waters of Niagara Falls were used to light homes in the nearby city of Buffalo.

Hydropower around the World

Since those early days, hydropower usage has grown all around the world. Today, about 19 percent—nearly one-fifth—of the world's electricity is generated this way. But this varies greatly from country to country. As you can see from the bar chart, hydroelectricity produces

TOP TEN HYDROELECTRIC PRODUCERS

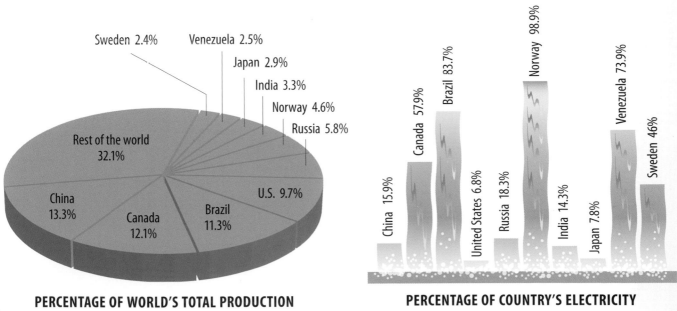

Sweden 2.4%   Venezuela 2.5%
Japan 2.9%
India 3.3%
Norway 4.6%
Russia 5.8%
Rest of the world 32.1%
U.S. 9.7%
China 13.3%
Canada 12.1%
Brazil 11.3%

PERCENTAGE OF WORLD'S TOTAL PRODUCTION

China 15.9%
Canada 57.9%
Brazil 83.7%
United States 6.8%
Russia 18.3%
Norway 98.9%
India 14.3%
Japan 7.8%
Venezuela 73.9%
Sweden 46%

PERCENTAGE OF COUNTRY'S ELECTRICITY

The Hoover Dam, on the Arizona-Nevada border, holds back the waters of the Colorado River. The reservoir behind the dam is Lake Mead. The dam feeds a powerful hydroelectric power plant.

nearly all of Norway's electricity, and a great deal of electricity in Brazil and Venezuela. The world's biggest producer of hydroelectric power is China (which also has the world's largest population). Even so, only 15.9 percent of China's electricity is produced from this source. Other sources, such as coal, produce more. The world's top five producing countries combined generate more than half the world's hydroelectricity.

Reservoirs and Dams

A hydroelectric dam across a river slows the natural flow of water and creates a reservoir. This reservoir provides a large store of water for making electricity. The reservoir is especially useful when there has been little rain and the river is low. However, if there are floods, spillways can be opened to let more water than usual flow through the dam and on down the river.

Are Dams Dangerous?

They can be, because they hold back huge volumes of water that would not naturally collect in one place. When the reservoir behind the 726 foot (221 m) high Hoover Dam was created in 1936, the weight of water caused earth tremors in the surrounding region. Fortunately, no damage was done to the dam. In 1963, there was a landslide into the reservoir behind the Vajont Dam in northern Italy. This caused a huge wave to burst over the dam, damaging the top, but not knocking it down. The water crashed down the valley and destroyed five villages, killing as many as 2,500 people.

WATER POWER

Turning the Turbines

Hydroelectric dams have channels called penstocks below the waterline of the reservoir. Water flows down each penstock by the force of gravity, heading toward the continuation of the river. As the water flows through the channel, it turns the blades of a turbine. This changes the kinetic energy of the water (which is produced by movement) into mechanical energy (which can power a machine). The blades are connected to a shaft, which also turns. After passing and turning the blades, the water flows on down the river. Storing huge volumes of water in the reservoir makes sure that the dam's turbines can turn constantly.

Four continents produce 96 percent of the world's hydroelectricity.

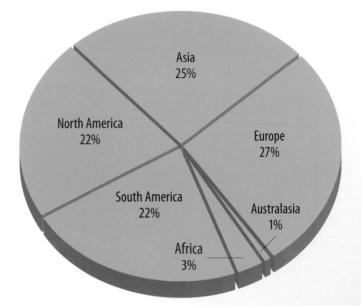

This cross section shows how water falling from the reservoir powers a turbine before passing on down the river.

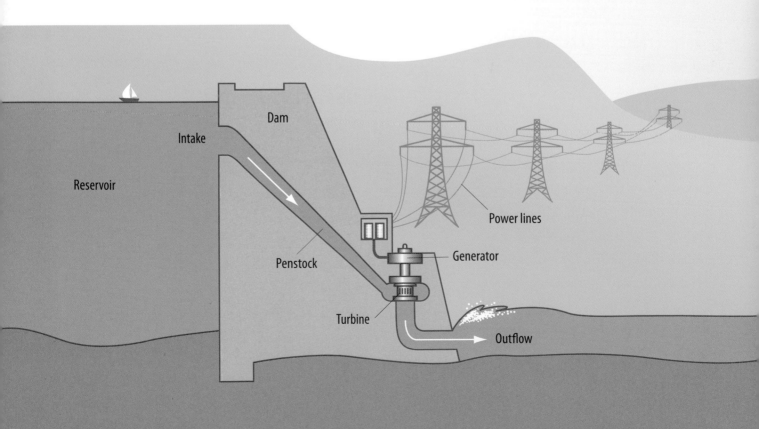

Generating Electricity

In 1831, British scientist Michael Faraday (1791–1867) discovered that he could create electricity by moving a magnet through a coil of copper wire. This process, called electromagnetic induction, led to the invention of the electric generator and electric motor.

Hydroelectric dams generate power by moving the turbine shaft, which is connected to a rotor that makes magnets spin inside wire coils. This turns mechanical energy into electrical energy. It is a very efficient process. Large generators can convert more than 90 percent of the turbine's mechanical energy into electrical energy. The rest (less than 10 percent) is converted into heat, so generators also have a cooling system to keep them from overheating.

Damming the Chang Jiang

The most powerful hydroelectric project in the world is being built on the Chang Jiang, China's longest river. Work on the concrete dam began in 1993, and the project is due to be completed during 2011. This enormous power plant will bring electricity to millions of Chinese villagers for the first time. The dam is also intended to help flood control in the region. However, it has had a huge impact on the local population. Approximately 2 million people have had to move from their homes as the land will be used for the reservoir.

The ancient town of Dachang was moved more than 3 miles (6 km) to avoid being flooded by the Three Gorges reservoir. New buildings are also going up.

A Threat to the Environment?

Hydro plants change the environment and can cause landslides, soil erosion, and water pollution. In 2007, the Chinese state media announced that 4 million more people would have to move because of the possibility that the Three Gorges Dam might cause "an environmental catastrophe." The buildup of silt in the reservoir reduces the amount of silt carried downstream and could cause more erosion and sinking of coastal areas. The environmental organization Greenpeace says: "Building large-scale hydropower plants can be polluting and damaging to surrounding ecosystems. Changing water supply can also have a detrimental effect on human communities, agriculture, and ecosystems further downstream. Hydro projects can also be unreliable during prolonged droughts and dry seasons when rivers dry up or reduce in volume."

Huge Hydro

The Three Gorges system is the second large dam on the Chang Jiang, after the Gezhouba Dam (completed in 1988), but China plans many more. It wants to almost triple its hydropower capacity by 2020, when it aims to produce 15 percent of its energy from renewable sources. China plans 12 hydropower bases further up the Chang Jiang, which will displace more people. China has suspended plans for 13 dams along the Nu River, in Yunnan province, which flows through the Three Parallel Rivers National Park. This is a World Heritage Site, which UNESCO says "may be the most biologically diverse temperate ecosystem in the world."

Storing Water Power

Many parts of the world have pumped storage plants. The storage station has two reservoirs, one higher than the other, usually on a mountainside. During the day when electricity demand is high, water flows down through pipes from the upper to the lower reservoir. The water turns turbine generators that produce electricity. When demand is low, the generators are reversed so they pump water up the pipes to the higher reservoir. Future storage stations may be combined with a wind or solar farm that could drive the pumps.

Three Gorges Dam Facts and Figures

Height: 607 feet (185 m)

Length: 1.45 miles (2.3 km)

Width: 377 feet (115 m) to 131 feet (40 m)

Concrete: 35.6 million cubic yards (27.2 million cu m)

Steel: 510,370 tons (463,000 t)

Reservoir: 410 miles (660 km) long; 574 feet (175 m) above sea level

Generators: 26 (plus 6 underground)

Generating capacity: 22,400 MW

Cost: official estimate at least $25 billion

The Three Gorges Dam is an enormous project. Experts welcome the use of renewable energy to supply China's increasingly huge need for electricity. Environmentalists fear that much damage is being caused to the region.

What Is a Watt?

A watt (W) is a unit of power that measures the rate of producing or using energy. The term was named after Scottish engineer James Watt (see page 12), who developed an improved steam engine. Watt measured his engine's performance in horsepower (hp). One horsepower equals 746 watts. Today, watts are generally used to measure electric power.

1 kilowatt (kW) = 1 thousand watts

1 megawatt (MW) = 1 million watts

1 gigawatt (GW) = 1 billion watts

Bath County Storage Station

One of the largest pumped storage plants began operating in the Allegheny Mountains of Virginia in 1985. The top reservoir is 1,263 feet (385 m) higher than the lower one. The Bath County station's six generators produce 2.1 GW of electricity—about one-tenth of that produced by the giant Three Gorges Dam.

The generator hall at the Raccoon Mountain pumped storage plant in Tennessee. The four generators produce 1.5 GW.

Hydro Plants and Greenhouse Gases

Hydropower does not produce greenhouse gases in the way that burning fossil fuels does. However, research has shown that large reservoirs—especially in tropical regions— give off methane and carbon dioxide (which are both greenhouse gases). This happens as plant material decays in the water. The World Energy Council says: "In terms of climate change, hydropower tends to have a very low greenhouse gas footprint. As water carries carbon in the natural cycle, scientists have investigated the extent to which a new reservoir might accelerate carbon emissions. In some very shallow tropical reservoirs, this may be the case, and the factor would need to be taken into consideration in the life-cycle analysis of such [systems]. In contrast, many reservoirs around the world have been monitored to test their emissions, confirming that hydropower is one of the cleanest methods of power generation."

Microhydro Systems

Small-scale systems are becoming popular in regions without a national electricity grid and in developing countries. Microhydro systems can produce electricity from rivers and streams for small communities. This form of hydropower has been growing at about 8 percent per year worldwide. Large-scale hydropower is growing at about 2 percent. One advantage of microhydro systems is that electricity can be produced very close to where it is used. This means that there is no need for transmission towers and the systems have little effect on the environment.

Serving the Community

Microhydro systems work well in mountainous areas, where streams run fast all year. They are being developed in countries such as Bhutan and Nepal, in the Himalayas, and on the island of Sri Lanka. In Nepal, farmers grow rice in terraced fields on steep hillsides. Some have installed small hydro-generators in the irrigation channels between their fields. Hydropower can replace fossil fuels by reducing the use of diesel engines and kerosene lamps. In China, the number of people using microhydro systems grew by 38 percent in one year (2005).

Aluminum Smelting

Some hydroelectric systems serve a particular industry. The best example is aluminum. One of the most successful methods of aluminum smelting (separating the metal from its rocky ore) uses huge amounts of electricity. In New Zealand and elsewhere, aluminum plants use energy supplied by nearby hydroelectric plants. Many such systems are controversial, however, because aluminum smelting produces huge amounts of pollution and emits large quantities of carbon dioxide. A new aluminum smelter in Iceland plans to use five dams and has been condemned by environmental groups. According to the Saving Iceland organization, the Kárahnjúkar Dam project risks destroying "Europe's largest remaining wilderness."

From Watermill to Microhydro

In Britain and elsewhere, micro systems are being installed to replace power from public utilities. Some farmers have set up their own small hydro-generators on streams that flow through their land. In some cases, the new generators replace old watermills. Some farmers have found that the new systems produce so much power that they are able to sell the surplus electricity they generate to their public power utilities.

The Tungu-Kabiri microhydro community project is in Mbuiru village, Kenya. Water in the channel drives a generator to produce 18 kW of electricity. The project has allowed the community to stop using diesel engines.

Is Hydro a Waste of Water?

Hydro systems do not waste the world's most precious resource, because the water they use is still there afterward. After turning turbines, the water flows downriver. Many hydroelectric dams and reservoirs are also used for irrigation. An example is the Hoover Dam (see page 15) on the Colorado River in the United States. The dam's generators provide electricity for much of Nevada, Arizona, and southern California. Water from its reservoir, Lake Mead, is used to irrigate approximately 1,545 square miles (4,000 sq km) of farmland. It also forms a recreation area that attracts up to 10 million visitors every year. Boating, swimming, and fishing are popular activities on the lake.

Generating Energy from Tides

Hundreds of years ago, there were tide mills along the Atlantic coasts of Europe and North America. Their waterwheels used the power of ocean tides rather than the fast-flowing water of a river.

Water flowed into a pond as the tide came in and the water level rose. After the tide had receded, the pond's water was released through a sluice and turned a waterwheel. Some tide mills still exist, but they are not used to generate much power. However, similar modern methods use the tides, and these will be used more in the future.

Harvesting Tides

There are several ways in which tidal power is harvested today. Three methods are already used, and others are being developed. They all use turbines beneath the surface of the water. The first method involves building a barrage across a tidal estuary. In the second, an offshore tidal lagoon is constructed. The third method uses tidal streams or currents.

This diagram shows the barrage at low tide in the estuary. At this time, the sluice gates can be opened to let water out of the basin. As it flows, the water turns the turbine.

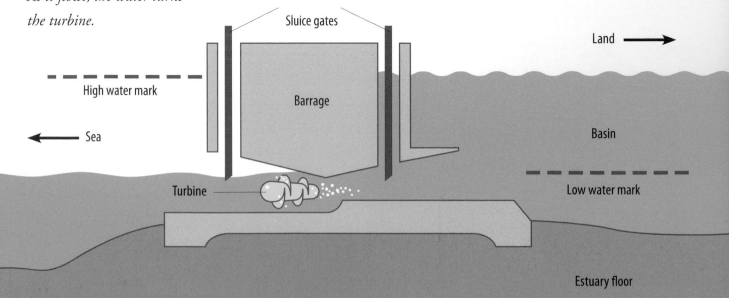

Barrage Technology

Tidal barrages work in a similar way to hydroelectric dams. A barrage is a long concrete barrier built across a wide estuary at the mouth of a river. The river water upstream of the barrage, called the basin, acts as a reservoir. The barrage has sluices to let water through and a series of turbines to power generators.

At low tide, the sluices are left open. As the tide comes in and water flows from the ocean into the estuary, the water level rises and the basin is filled through the sluices. Then the sluice gates are closed. In some systems, the turbines are used in reverse to pump even more water into the basin. Other systems keep the turbine gates closed until the tide has gone out again. When the sea level has fallen, a drop is created between the basin and the sea. Then the turbine gates are opened so that ebbing water flows through them. This process is called ebb or outflow generation.

In some systems, the turbines are powered by the rising flood tide as well. This flood or inflow generation is much less efficient than ebb generation, because the water is not moving as fast and does not have as much power.

Barrages and the Environment

Environmentalists are interested in tidal barrages because, apart from building the barrage, greenhouse gases are not produced. But they are also concerned because building a barrage has an effect on the nearby coastline, especially the area that is covered at high tide and exposed at low tide (the intertidal habitat).

Rivers and estuaries carry a large amount of sediment to the sea, and barrages can affect this, leading to a buildup of sediment within the basin. Jonathon Porrit, chairman of the Sustainable Development Commission, says: "The potential for [a tidal barrage] to reduce carbon emissions and improve energy security needs to be balanced against the impact on the estuary's unique habitat, as well as communities and businesses."

Energy experts have learned a great deal about the benefits and problems of tidal barrages from the Rance barrage in northern France.

Allowing Boats Through

Tidal barrages and many hydroelectric dams have locks to allow ships to pass beyond the barrier. A 1,092 foot (333 m) long barrage on the Rance River, in northern France, became the world's first working tidal power plant in 1966. Its 24 turbines produce 240 MW of electricity— about one-fourth as much as a coal-fired power station (and just over 1 percent of the electricity generated by the Three Gorges Dam). The Rance barrage has a lock at one side of the estuary that allows boats to pass to and from the river to the English Channel. Approximately 16,000 vessels pass through the lock every year.

The Severn Estuary Project

The Severn is the longest river in Britain. Its estuary has one of the largest tidal ranges in the world (an average of 43 feet (13 m) between high and low tide). The first plans to build a barrage across the estuary between South Wales and southwest England were drawn up in 1925. The cost then was too high, and this is still a consideration today. A Severn Barrage Committee was set up in 1981, and many plans have been put forward.

The latest plan is to build a 10 mile (16 km) long barrage with 200–300 turbines. This would generate more than 8,000 MW (at least 33 times more than the Rance barrage), providing nearly 5 percent of Britain's electricity. In 2007, planners said that the barrage could be producing electricity in 11 years. In the meantime, the British government has ordered another study.

The Impact on Wildlife

The mudflats, salt marshes, and rocky islands of the Severn Estuary are host to about 65,000 migratory birds in winter. The Wildfowl and Wetlands Trust runs the Slimbridge Wetland Refuge on the banks of the Severn. Its director says consideration must be given to the wildlife: "The Severn Estuary is one of the UK's [United Kingdom's] most important sites for water birds... The construction of a huge dam across the estuary could have a massive environmental impact on this delicate ecosystem and the wildlife that depends on it... It would be far better to spend the £15 to £20 billion [$26 to $35 billion] the barrage will cost on measures that will cut emissions more quickly. The Severn Estuary is an irreplaceable refuge for wildlife."

Thousands of birds and fish would be put at risk. A number of sites protected by UK, international, and European law would be damaged by a barrage. This map shows these sites, as well as the site of the proposed barrage.

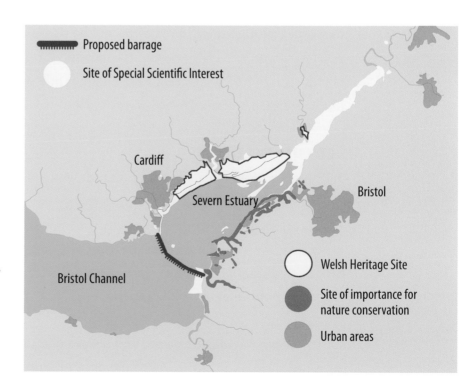

This map shows the many conservation sites along the banks of the Severn. These could be affected by the proposed barrage.

Tidal Lagoons

Many experts believe that dams and barrages will be replaced by tidal lagoons. The lagoon is created by a circular wall built in the shallow waters of a coastal bay. Turbines are placed in the wall at regular intervals. They turn as water flows into and out of the lagoon with the tides. The tidal lagoon proposed for Swansea Bay in South Wales will be about 1 mile (1.6 km) offshore and cover about 2 square miles (5 sq km) of sea. The lagoon wall will stand about 3 feet (1 m) above the surface at high tide. The turbines will be two-directional and generate about 30 MW of electricity—enough for up to 10,000 homes—on both the incoming and outgoing tide. The tidal range in this location is about 26 feet (8 m).

Currents or Streams

Scientific environmentalist James Lovelock wrote in 2006, "While such schemes [that aim to draw energy from the movements of the sea] seem well worthwhile as experiments and to gain hands-on experience, we should not expect even the most promising of them to deliver a substantial part of our energy needs before at least twenty, and more probably forty, years have passed."

Other scientists strongly disagree and believe that using tidal currents (also called tidal streams) is one of the most promising forms of

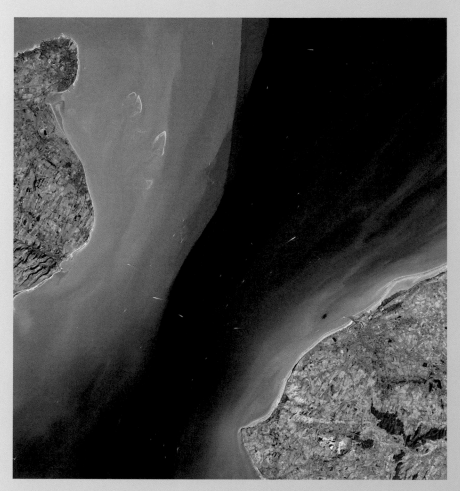

This satellite image shows tidal currents in the Strait of Dover, the narrowest part of the English Channel.

energy generation for the future. Currents are often strongest in narrow straits between islands and around headlands near the coast. Their speed is usually highest at mid ebb and mid flood (that is, halfway between high and low tide). The moving water of currents can power turbines in the same way that moving air powers windmills.

Lagoons versus Barrages

Lagoons are more environmentally friendly than barrages because they have less effect on coastal mudflats and the intertidal region. Barrages reduce the saltiness of the water in the basin, because it mingles less with the seawater. However, there are environmental problems with lagoons, and they also interfere with shipping and leisure activities. The environmental group Friends of the Earth has conducted several studies and concluded that lagoons are a better option than barrages. The group has suggested that a number of lagoons in the Severn Estuary would be more effective and better for the environment than one large barrage.

Yalu Dam and Lagoon

The Yalu River forms much of the border between China and North Korea before emptying into Korea Bay. There is already a large hydroelectric dam on the river near Sinuiju, North Korea (where the river is called Amnok). Now there are plans to build a tidal lagoon in the bay near the mouth of the river. The project aims to generate 300 MW of electricity—10 times as much as the Swansea project.

Underwater Rotors

The East River is a tidal strait in New York City. The strait connects Long Island Sound to the north to Upper New York Bay at its south end, separating Manhattan from Long Island. As part of the Roosevelt Island Tidal Energy (RITE) project, the first tidal turbine was installed beside an island in the river in 2006.

Each RITE turbine is 20 feet (6 m) high. The rotor is 16 feet (5 m) in diameter, and a generator produces 35 kW. The turbines are anchored to the bottom of the strait, which has an average depth of 30 feet (9 m). The first turbine generates enough electricity for 16 New York homes. By 2010, the energy company operating the site hopes to have 200–300 turbines beside Roosevelt Island, forming a tidal farm and generating up to 10 MW of electricity.

The turbine rotor blades turn very slowly (up to 32 revolutions per minute), and the company claims that not a single fish has been killed by a turbine. There has also been no sign of environmental damage. This tidal energy is produced within close proximity to the United Nations headquarters in North America's largest city.

Opposite: Two of the RITE turbines are ready to be lowered into the East River off Manhattan.

Twin Blades

Other rotors are larger and more powerful. The SeaGen turbine has twin rotors measuring about 50–60 feet (15–20 m) in diameter. These are mounted on the wing-like extensions of a steel pile set into a hole drilled in the seabed. In 2008, the first of these large turbines was set up in the tidal narrows of Strangford Lough, an inlet of the Irish Sea in Northern Ireland. This inlet has one of the fastest tidal flows in the world, and the turbine will be able to produce 1.2 MW of electricity. That is enough to power 1,000 homes.

Exploiting the Sea

The company developing the SeaGen turbine says: "Our technology represents a novel method for generating electricity from a huge energy resource in the sea. It is rare for an entirely new energy resource to be developed but even rarer if the technology:
• produces no pollution and has negligible environmental impact;
• delivers energy to a predictable timetable;
• has the potential to make a major contribution to energy needs.
Although the relentless energy of marine currents has been obvious from the earliest days of seafaring, it is only now that. . . modern offshore engineering. . . coinciding with the need to find large new renewable energy resources makes this a technically. . . and economically viable possibility."

Power All the Time?

Turbines should be able to generate power all the time, but this depends on where they are. The RITE project claims its turbines produce electricity 77 percent of the time. One limiting factor is the variation in tidal stream power as the tides change throughout a month.

This chart shows different levels of power generated over 13 days. Days 1 and 13 had the highest spring tides, while day 7 had the lowest neap tides.

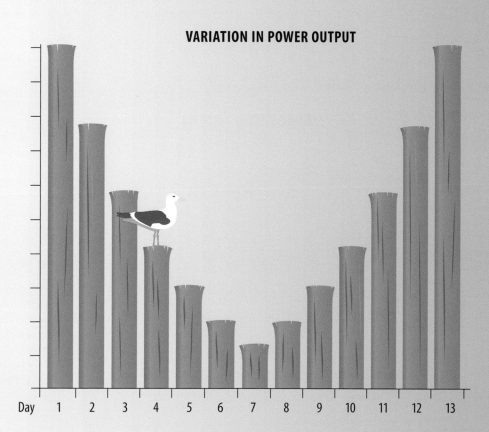

VARIATION IN POWER OUTPUT

Day 1 2 3 4 5 6 7 8 9 10 11 12 13

Harnessing the Waves

The ocean is constantly moving, as the wind blows over its surface and creates powerful waves.

As with other forms of water power, this mechanical energy can be turned into electrical energy. Scientists and inventors have visualized all sorts of different devices to harvest wave power, and many of them are now being put into action.

Powerful Sea Snakes

One successful modern development, Pelamis, is named after a sea snake. A steel Pelamis wave energy converter is about 490 feet (150 m) long and 11.5 feet (3.5 m) wide. It is designed to be moored about 3–6 miles (5–10 km) from the shore in waters about 165–230 feet (50–70 m) deep. The British manufacturers believe that this is where "the high energy levels found in deep swell waves can be accessed."

A Pelamis has four cylindrical sections linked by three hinged joints. Waves make the joints move, pushing and pulling hydraulic rams that force high-pressure fluid through motors to drive electric generators. The electricity flows down a cable to the seabed and then to land. In 2008, three of these mechanical sea snakes were set up off the coast of

Nodding Ducks

During the 1970s, scientists and engineers at the University of Edinburgh developed and tested devices that floated on water, moved with the waves, and turned that movement into electrical power. These early devices, called nodding ducks, were a series of hinged flaps that bobbed up and down. They led to many of the wave devices that are now being developed.

Will Wave Farms Alter Waves?

They will have little effect, according to some studies. But we will not really know until large wave farms start to operate. One manufacturer claims that its wave converters "may reduce shoreline erosion." This suggests that they will reduce waves. One concerned group is the surfing community. Surfers fear that wave farms will reduce the height of waves as they reach the shore and are protesting. The Surfer's Path web site says: "Suddenly surfers are being seen as the ones standing in the way of progress because they don't want to give up their luxuries for the benefit of the rest of society. The luxuries in question aren't cars, intercontinental flights or seaside properties, but the very waves we ride. . . So now it's not so clear who the 'baddies' really are. In general, surfers are normally the ones campaigning against environmental villains such as polluters and coastal developers. Now, for this group of protesters, environmentalists are the 'enemy.'"

Portugal to form the world's first commercial wave farm. Eventually the company would like to have several hundred snakes that could produce 500 MW of electricity. The Portuguese government supports the plan. The country's renewable energy target for 2010 has increased from 39 to 45 percent.

The arrows show how the hinged joints of a Pelamis wave energy converter move on the waves.

PELAMIS WAVE FARM

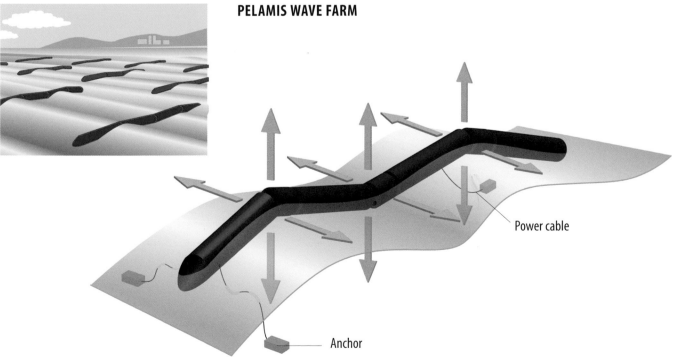

Power cable

Anchor

How Much Power?

An offshore wave farm of 40 Pelamis machines would cover 0.4 square miles (1 sq km) of ocean and generate 30 MW of electricity—enough power for 20,000 homes. But it would not produce greenhouse gases. In a year, every Pelamis could prevent 2,204 tons (2,000 t) of carbon dioxide entering the atmosphere. This is the amount of carbon dioxide a gas turbine would emit when generating the same amount of electricity. This is also true of other wave energy converters. They are all modular and can be joined together in different patterns to increase their number and power.

Bouncing Buoys

Other manufacturers are generating electricity from the movement of ocean buoys. Engineers have found several different ways of making this work.

Ocean Power Technologies' PowerBuoy has been tested in both the Atlantic and Pacific oceans.

Popular with People

An objection to most forms of energy production is the NIMBY (not in my back yard) attitude. People do not want power plants to spoil their neighborhoods or the views from their windows. Will people worry about their view of the ocean? The manufacturers think not. A 10 MW PowerBuoy wave farm takes up just 0.048 square miles (0.125 sq km) of ocean. The manufacturer is installing a small wave farm off the northern coast of Spain. It says: "Only a small portion of the buoy is visible at close range, with the bulk of the buoy hidden below the water. Since an OPT wave power station is typically located 1–3 miles [1.6–4.8 km] offshore, the PowerBuoys are usually not visible from the shore."

Other companies say the same: "A cluster of AquaBuoys would have a low silhouette in the water. Located several miles offshore, the power plant arrays would be visible to allow for safe navigation and no more noticeable than a small fishing fleet."

The American 4.9 foot (1.5 m) wide PowerBuoy has a central 29.5 foot (9 m) long column. Around it, a moving float lifts rods in and out of the center of the column, driving a generator. The Canadian AquaBuoy is a 10 foot (3 m) wide buoy that works differently. It is tied to a 69 foot (21 m) long underwater shaft. As the buoy bobs up and down, water rushes into a tube in the shaft and causes a piston to move. The moving piston stretches a steel-reinforced rubber hose, which pumps the water into a turbine that powers a generator.

A Danish Alternative

A Danish company has devised a Wave Dragon, known as an overtopping device. Reflectors, or arms, guide water up a ramp and into a reservoir above sea level. This water is then let out into the sea through turbines connected to electric generators. The Wave Dragon is simple in construction and has only one moving part—the turbine. It is similar to an isolated hydroelectric plant out at sea.

The first Wave Dragon overtopping converter was tested in the North Sea off the coast of Denmark.

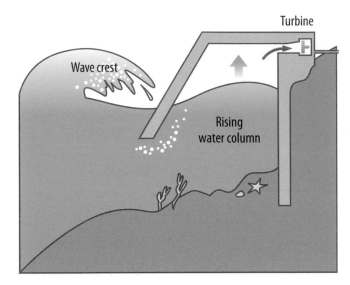

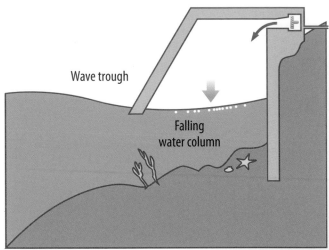

In an onshore OWC generator, air is forced up through a turbine by the rising water of the waves.

Onshore Wave Stations

LIMPET (Land Installed Marine Powered Energy Transformer) is a shore-based wave station on the island of Islay, off Scotland's west coast. The station was installed in 2000 and produces power for the national power grid.

A LIMPET has a sloping shell built into rocks on the shore. It has an inlet big enough to allow seawater waves to splash into a chamber. When they do this, the level of water rises and acts as a piston, pushing air to the top of the chamber. The air is forced through a gap into a turbine, which turns in the direction of airflow. As the water inside the chamber falls again before the next wave hits, air is sucked back into the chamber and keeps the turbine blades turning. This system works on the oscillating water column (OWC) principle.

The Islay Wave Bus

The environmental organization Greenpeace runs a bus on electricity generated by the LIMPET station on the island of Islay. This is the first electric bus in the world to be powered by wave energy. It is used by local community groups. The bus's batteries are recharged every night with electricity supplied by the wave station. The bus's fuel cost is about one-third of buses that run on diesel.

Greenpeace says: "The wave bus doesn't fill up on petrol or diesel, so will emit no exhaust pollution, meaning a minimal local environmental impact. This feature is common to all electric vehicles, but when the electricity used to recharge them comes from a renewable energy source—such as the waves, wind, or sun—the electricity generating process does not produce carbon dioxide, the main cause of global warming."

Seawater Pumps

A different wave energy system uses buoys tethered just beneath the surface of the sea. This system can pump seawater to shore using wave-induced movement. The pumped seawater then either turns the blades of a hydro-turbine or powers a desalination unit to produce fresh water. This is called a CETO (Cylindrical Energy Transfer Oscillating) system. It has been successfully tested in Australia.

A simple diagram of the CETO pumping system

Desalinated water

Turbine and generator

Pressurized seawater

A Global Resource?

Some of the world's coasts are more suitable for harnessing wave power than others. All around the world, the coastlines with the most potential for wave power generally face west. These include coastlines in South Australia, New Zealand, Iceland, southern Chile, Ireland, and Scotland, as well as parts of western Canada and South Africa. Wave projects are also being developed on the Pacific coast of the United States.

Many islands in the Pacific Ocean have the potential to generate wave power, because their wave energy is steady in both strength and direction. The World Energy Council estimates that twice the amount of electricity than is currently supplied by wave energy could be generated around the world. That is the same as the electricity produced by 2,000 large oil, gas, coal, or nuclear power stations.

Using the Ocean Depths

The world's oceans are a vast renewable resource, with the potential to help us produce huge amounts of electric power. In addition to tidal and wave power, another technology has great potential.

Ocean thermal energy conversion (OTEC) uses temperature differences in the layers of water in the oceans to generate power, including electricity. With a temperature difference of about 36°F (20°C) between an ocean's warm surface water and its cold deep water, an OTEC system can produce significant amounts of power.

The greatest differences in water temperature are in tropical regions near the equator, such as to the north and east of Indonesia. These regions are best for OTEC.

Developing Ideas

As with other forms of water power, OTEC is not an entirely new technology. French physician and physicist Arsène d'Arsonval (1851–1940) was the first scientist to suggest harvesting the thermal energy of the ocean, in 1881. Forty-nine years later, one of his students, Georges

WATER TEMPERATURE DIFFERENCE BETWEEN SURFACE AND DEPTH OF 3,280 FEET (1,000 M)

Less than 33°F (18°C)

36° to 40°F (20° to 22°C)

More than 43°F (24°C)

33° to 36°F (18° to 20°C)

40° to 43°F (22° to 24°C)

Depth less than 3,280 feet (1,000 m)

Claude (1870–1960), built a working OTEC plant. His prototype produced 22 kW of electricity, using ocean waters off Cuba. He built another plant on a ship moored off the coast of Brazil in 1935, but this was destroyed during stormy weather.

Exchanging Heat

An OTEC system works similar to a refrigeration unit in reverse. Warm surface seawater is pumped through a heat exchanger, where a refrigeration fluid boils and turns to vapor. The expanding vapor drives a turbine. At the same time, cold seawater is pumped from the depths of the ocean to cool the vapor and turn it back into a liquid. This is then recycled through the system. The turbine drives a generator, and the resulting electricity is sent to shore through an underwater cable. This is called a closed-cycle OTEC system.

An Enormous Resource

The U.S. National Renewable Energy Laboratory has this to say about OTEC technology: "The oceans cover a little more than 70 percent of Earth's surface. This makes them the world's largest solar energy collector and energy storage system. On an average day, 60 million square kilometers (23 million square miles) of tropical seas absorb an amount of solar radiation equal in heat content to about 250 billion barrels of oil. If less than one-tenth of 1 percent of this stored solar energy could be converted into electric power, it would supply more than 20 times the total amount of electricity consumed in the United States on any given day."

Expensive Technology

OTEC power plants are very expensive to develop and build. They involve a huge investment, so national governments need to offer financial incentives to private companies. This may happen when the price of electricity from other sources, especially fossil fuels, rises beyond a certain level. In 1956, French scientists designed a 3 MW plant to be based at the West African seaport of Abidjan, then the capital of the French colony of Côte d'Ivoire. But the plant was never finished because hydroelectric power proved to be much cheaper. Another disadvantage is that there may not be very many suitable land-based sites in the tropics where deep-ocean water is close enough to shore to make OTEC plants practical.

A Record-breaking System

An open-cycle OTEC system uses warm surface water as the working fluid. The water vaporizes in a near vacuum, and the expanding vapor drives a turbine. The vapor, which has lost its salt and is almost pure fresh water, is condensed back into a liquid by exposure to cold temperatures from deep ocean water. If the condenser keeps the vapor from direct contact with seawater, the condensed fresh water can be used for drinking, irrigation, or aquaculture. This open system is also known as the Claude Cycle, after its inventor Georges Claude. In 1993, a 210 kW open-cycle plant was built in Hawaii. It set a world record for OTEC power production at 255 kW.

What Can OTEC Do?

As well as generating electricity, OTEC systems can be used to desalinate water, run refrigeration and air-conditioning units, and help the growth of marine organisms and plant life near shore or on land. OTEC can also be used to produce methanol, ammonia, hydrogen, aluminum, chlorine, and other chemicals.

Tropical Locations

To work well, an OTEC system needs ocean temperature differences as found in the tropics (see the map on page 36), just north and south of the equator. Many tropical islands need more energy and presently depend on expensive imported oil. These islands would be ideal areas for OTEC systems.

Hawaiian Development

Most OTEC research has occured in Hawaii, where the United States set up a Natural Energy Laboratory in 1974. By 1979, a converted U.S. Navy barge produced 50 kW of electricity by the OTEC method. The Keahole Point location is ideal because there is a steep shelf just offshore. Today, an OTEC plant onshore receives 43°F (6°C) cold seawater from almost 2,000 feet (600 m) below the surface through a pipeline. The surface water temperature varies between 76° and 81.5°F (24.5° and 27.5°C). This plant is used for air conditioning and refrigeration.

The onshore OTEC plant at Keahole Point, Hawaii

Are There Environmental Problems?

An expert wrote in the trade magazine *OTEC News*: "The flow of water from a 100 MW OTEC plant would equal that of a major river—equivalent to the nominal flow of the Colorado River into the Pacific Ocean. In fact, the discharge flow from 60,000 MW (0.6 percent of present world consumption) of OTEC plants would be equivalent to the combined discharge from all the rivers flowing into the Atlantic and Pacific oceans." Experts believe that changes in the temperature and salinity of the water will have little impact on life in the oceans. Environmental scientist Rick Dworsky writes in *Energy Bulletin*: "It may well be the case that OTEC can target some of the energy that causes damaging and catastrophic storms and redirect it into useful work, if large mobile floating platforms become a reality. . . OTEC appears to be a vast, renewable, sustainable, safe, 'always on' energy source that does not emit CO_2 [carbon dioxide] or nuclear waste."

What Does the Future Hold?

Hydropower is becoming recognized as an important source of energy. This growth in interest and development is expected to continue as environmental groups put pressure on politicians and business leaders to use more renewable energy.

According to a report by the United Nations Environment Programme, the use of hydropower will grow by 74 percent by 2030. During this period, the world's total energy requirement is expected to grow by 37 percent.

Hydropower and Global Warming

Earth's atmosphere prevents some of the Sun's rays from reaching Earth. Its gases also stop some heat escaping from Earth, just as glass traps warmth inside a greenhouse. We are adding to this natural greenhouse effect by emitting so many waste gases from power plants, factories, and cars. Many of these greenhouse gases—

Making the Case for Hydropower

Associations around the world aim to promote individual energy sources so that they gain public support. In the United States, the National Hydropower Association presents its case in this way: "Hydropower is a domestic source of clean, renewable, reliable, and affordable electricity. It is more than electricity. Hydropower also provides recreational enhancements, flood control, and irrigation. It is an extremely important energy source that has significant growth opportunity in helping the nation meet new energy supply with a reliable and low-emitting, home-grown energy source. Hydropower is clean energy for a secure future."

Do you think this is a convincing argument?

especially carbon dioxide—are produced when we burn coal, oil, or gas to release energy. Experts have discovered that, in this way, humans are making natural climate change more extreme. Much of our energy use adds to global warming that gradually increases land, sea, and air temperatures. Using energy from renewable energy sources can help to reduce the increase in global warming. Hydropower will continue to play an important part in this.

New Systems?

New kinds of wave energy converters are being invented, and scientists continue to work on using the oceans' enormous energy potential. Perhaps, completely new systems will be discovered. It is also possible that offshore wave and tide facilities could combine with wind farms to make even more powerful renewable power plants.

Opposite: This satellite image shows ice coverage in the Arctic Ocean in September 2007. Since 1980, this ice mass has been shrinking by nearly 1 percent every year. Scientists say that global warming is causing polar ice to melt.

Fair Energy Prices

Germany and other countries have a system called a feed-in tariff. This is the price per unit of electricity that a national or regional energy supplier pays for renewable electricity (including hydro) from private generators. The government regulates the tariff (or price). In Germany, this is covered by a Renewable Energy Law that is updated regularly.

The law aims to help new energy-generating companies to start operating and to compete with established suppliers that burn mainly fossil fuels. It also encourages investors to contribute to the cost of setting up hydro systems, which can be very expensive. Once the costs of setup have been paid, the energy supplied should be very cheap, and, of course, environmentally friendly.

Hydropower for Industry

Many rich, industrialized countries will increase their production of hydropower in the future. Norway is mountainous and has a long coastline. Its high rainfall, rivers, and waterfalls are ideal for hydropower, which provides nearly all Norway's electricity (see page 14). Because of this, Norway exports all the gas and most of the oil it recovers offshore in the North Sea. This makes Norway the world's fifth-largest oil exporter and third-largest gas exporter. Norway has more than 70 large hydroelectric power plants and many more smaller ones. Norwegian scientists are also testing wave generators off the coast.

Oslo is the capital and largest city of Norway. As in other Norwegian cities, its electricity comes mainly from hydropower.

The Developing World

Many developing countries will use more microhydro systems. Nepal, for example, has no coastline but many rivers flowing south towards India. An estimated 1 percent of Nepal's hydroelectric potential currently is tapped.

Laos, in South East Asia, is another poor, mountainous, landlocked country. The Mekong River flows through Laos, and the river's tributaries offer huge potential for generating hydroelectric power. The Laos government plans to construct a huge dam

Water-Powered Cars and Batteries?

Scientists and inventors claim to have found ways to use water to power cars, but none has been commercially developed. The concept is to use water with the chemical element boron, as a source of hydrogen fuel. A report in *New Scientist* magazine in August 2006 stated: "The team calculates that a car would have to carry just 18 kilograms [40 pounds] of boron and 45 liters [12 gallons] of water to produce 5 kilograms [11 pounds] of hydrogen, which has the same energy content as a 40-liter [10.5 gallon] tank of conventional fuel. An Israeli company is designing a prototype engine that works in the same way, and the Japanese company Samsung has built a prototype scooter based on a similar idea." Other inventors have worked on adding water to carbon-based compounds in small batteries for powering cell phones, flashlights, and other electronic devices.

on the Nam Theun tributary. Neighboring China, Thailand, and Vietnam all want to import electricity from Laos, and Thailand hopes to take 90 percent of it. This huge project will cost $1.5 billion. The dam and plant are being built by a group of companies from France, Thailand, and Laos, backed by the World Bank and the Asian Development Bank. The project is scheduled for completion in 2009.

The Nam Theun Dam in Laos is under construction. The power plant will generate more than 1000 MW of electricity.

Which Form of Water Power Is Best?

You have to consider the pros and cons in every situation. Large hydroelectric dam systems are very effective and provide other benefits, such as water supply and flood control. But they can have an environmental and social impact.

Microhydro systems may be ideal for small communities. Supporters of tidal barrages need to convince opponents that they will not harm the local environment. This might depend on the location and the size of the barrier. Developments in wave energy conversion look promising, especially to countries with long coastlines. The potential for OTEC (see pages 36–39) is huge in tropical regions but needs much more (and expensive) development.

Glossary

aqueduct A channel built to carry water.

barrage A barrier built across a river or an estuary to prevent flooding or provide power.

biomass All plant and animal matter, especially when used as a fuel.

carbon dioxide (CO_2) A greenhouse gas given off when fossil fuels burn.

condenser A device that changes a gas into a liquid.

ebb The movement of a tide away from the land, creating low tide.

ecosystem A group of living things that depend on each other and their environment.

electrical energy Electricity (a form of energy that can be sent to our homes along cables).

emission Producing and giving off something (such as a waste gas); also, the waste gas produced and given off.

footprint The coverage, effect, or amount of something (such as a greenhouse gas).

fossil fuel A fuel (such as coal, oil, or natural gas) that comes from the remains of prehistoric plants and animals.

geothermal power Power produced by heat inside Earth.

global warming Heating up of Earth's surface, especially caused by pollution from burning fossil fuels.

greenhouse gas A gas, such as carbon dioxide, that traps heat from the Sun near Earth and helps to create the greenhouse effect.

habitat The natural home or environment of an animal or a plant.

heat exchanger A device that transfers heat from one substance to another.

hydroelectricity or hydropower Electricity generated using water power.

intertidal region An area covered by water at high tide and exposed to the air at low tide.

irrigation Watering the land, especially to help crops grow.

kinetic energy Energy produced by movement.

lagoon A coastal stretch of shallow water that is sometimes cut off from the sea.

mechanical energy The energy that something has because of its position (potential energy) and its movement (kinetic energy). Also, the energy transmitted by a machine.

methane A flammable gas that is the main element in natural gas.

national grid A country's network of electric power lines.

neap tide A tide that has a small range between its high and low water marks.

nonrenewable energy Energy that is used up and cannot be replaced (from sources such as coal, gas, oil, or uranium).

nuclear power Power produced by the energy inside atoms.

penstock A channel through which water flows from a reservoir to a dam's turbine.

renewable energy Sources of energy that do not run out by being used, such as biomass, geothermal, solar, water, and wind.

rotor The spinning assembly and blades of a turbine.

sediment Material worn away from rocks that is carried along by moving water and then deposited.

sluice A floodgate that controls water in a channel (letting it in or out).

spring tide A tide that has a large range between its high and low water marks.

strait A narrow body of water that links two larger seas.

sustainable development Economic growth that does not use up too many natural resources or pollute the environment.

thermal energy The power of heat.

tidal range The distance between the highest and lowest tide levels in a place.

turbine A machine with rotating blades that turn a shaft.

water cycle (or hydrological cycle) The constant, never-ending circulation of water between the air, land, and sea.

Web Sites

A History of Water Power

www.waterhistory.org/histories/waterwheels/

BBC Reports: Water Power and Tidal Power Plan for Swansea Bay

www.bbc.co.uk/climate/adaptation/water.shtml

http://news.bbc.co.uk/1/hi/wales/south_west/3234548.stm

Information on Ocean Thermal Energy Conversion (OTEC)

www.otecnews.org

www.oceansatlas.com/unatlas/uses/EnergyResources/Background/OTEC/OTEC2.html

Information on the PowerBuoy with a Link to a Discovery Channel Video

www.oceanpowertechnologies.com

Index